ENGLISH
TO
ENGLISH

ENGLISH

TO

ENGLISH

The A to Z of British-American Translations

COMPILED BY
SUZAN ST MAUR

HowToWriteBetter.net
©Suzan St Maur 2012

bookshaker

First Published In Great Britain 2012
by www.BookShaker.com

© Copyright Suzan St Maur

CONTENTS

ACKNOWLEDGEMENTS

Alyson Hercus

Angela Boothroyd
http://www.studyingonline.co.uk/

Jonathon Green
http://jonathongreen.co.uk

Linda Mattacks
http://www.smallbusinesstraining.co.uk/

Rhiannon Hill
http://www.brightonhovecounselling.co.uk/

Sarah Arrow
http://saraharrow.co.uk

...plus my other friends and family who, like the above, have helped supply some of these weird and wonderful terms.

To my cousin Keigan

*...hope this is helpful for your
excellent fiction writing. xx*

FOREWORD

By Jonathon Green
world-famous lexicographer
and expert in English slang

We should all, of course, be talking American by now. It is, after all, the basis of 'world English' and this is a global civilization, where the ever-expanding Internet communicates largely in American English and our popular culture, enjoyed by everyone, English-speaking or otherwise, dances to a Stateside tune. Nowhere more so than in the world I know best – English-language slang – where we have been using more and more American words since World War II and where, today, it seems that the under-thirties, irrespective of nationality or colour, all talk like a teenage black American.

Yet of course we don't. English English remains the mother tongue, and if we actually live in the UK, that is still what we talk. The language changes, it has been changing since Anglo-Saxon was replaced by Anglo-Norman and the various regional dialects had to give way to that of ever-dominant London, the language that became known as 'standard English'. Not everyone talks 'standard', not everyone opts for 'received pronunciation' or what used to be called 'BBC English', but in the end we still speak, in every sense, with an English accent. Meanwhile, three thousand miles to the west, they do things their way.

When, in 1776 the US declared its independence, the ex-colonists were still talking pretty much in the way they would have done had they or their grandparents stayed at home. But a new country requires a new language, or at least a version of an older one, and Americans were quick off the mark.

The lexicographer Noah Webster, whose great *Dictionary* appeared in 1828 and who in 1789 had been the first to use the phrase 'the American language', was determined to push the project forward. As well as collecting and explaining words, he created a whole new mode of spelling: it was not just a simplified, and what he saw as more practical version of the UK's notoriously problematic system, but a reflection of a new world, not to be tied to old and outmoded European habits. It is to Webster that we owe such differences as *center/centre*, *flavor/flavour*, *check/cheque*, the dropping of the second 'l' in words like 'traveled' and so on. On occasion his enthusiasm took him over the top, such as *tung* for tongue and *ake* for ache, and much would be dropped, but the change had come and would not go away.

Since then, at least in their standard speech, the two nations have moved apart. As the lists that follow make clear, Oscar Wilde's oft-quoted suggestion that they are 'separated by a common language' still holds true. It may be that we understand each other a little better –

on the whole we don't need subtitles to enjoy each other's TV shows and movies – and the days of re-editing our respective novels to replace 'different' words are mainly gone, but the gap remains.

And that gap can lead to embarrassment. It is not just a matter of setting one's spell-checker and keyboard to US or UK English. The blushing American woman, seconded to the London office, and asked if she has a *rubber* (US = condom / UK = eraser), her opposite number the stiff-upper-lipped Brit executive in New York, who is asked whether she wears *pants* (US = trousers / UK knickers, though knickers is also a problem: it means shorts in the US) to work. Slang may be increasingly international but it too has its pitfalls. The American *bum* is something very different in Britain: the former a tramp, the other the human posterior. Sometimes the words just don't travel, such as US *fall* for UK autumn, although 'fall of the leaf', its origin, was once used in 16th century England.

Difference, of course, can enliven. America and Britain are very different, for all that the original colonists were in part British-born. The UK has its immigrants, but their arrival has never created anything like the great American melting pot, still boiling as urgently as ever. Why not have alternative vocabularies. It is necessary, however, to remember that alternative can also mean other.

So let me commend what follows as an invaluable guide to possible, indeed probable pitfalls. And if I may return to slang, let me quote the English dictionary-maker, Elisha Coles, in 1676 the first to put that dangerous and exciting language into a standard dictionary: 'Tis no Disparagement to understand the Canting Terms: It may chance to save your Throat from being cut, or (at least) your Pocket from being pick'd.' We have moved on, or so one hopes, but forewarned is indeed forearmed, and that goes for language too, on whichever side of the Atlantic you may be standing.

Jonathon Green
www.jonathongreen.co.uk

INTRODUCTION:

WHY I COMPILED THIS BOOK

I'm a Canadian who lives in the UK. Every time I go "home" to Canada I'm obliged to change my vocabulary over from (British) to **North American**. (Yes, and back again when I return.) But on the way out there...

...After we have (disembarked) **deplaned**, I put my suitcases in the (boot) **trunk** of my (hire car) **rental car**, check that it has a full tank of (petrol) **gas**, open the (bonnet) **hood** and check there's plenty of oil in the (engine) **motor**, drive along the (motorway) **highway** and (turn right) **make a right** at the (junction) **4-way stop** to my family's home, (reverse) **back up** and park on the (drive) **driveway**, walk across the (fitted carpet) **broadloom** in the hall to the kitchen where my aunt puts a kettle on the (cooker) **stove** to make tea in cups she gets out of the (sideboard) **buffet**. Later I put my clothes away in the (wardrobe) **closet**, close the (curtains) **drapes**, then curl up in a lovely (quilt) **comforter** and go to sleep in a nice warm house heated by a powerful (boiler) **furnace**.

When I do a workshop there I (take the underground) **ride the subway** into the city, where – having previously (booked) **made reservations** I check into my hotel (accommodation) **accommodations** and agree to (full board) **American plan** for my stay. I go to my (meeting room) **business suite**, make a call or two on my (mobile phone) **cell phone**, and go through my (presentation) **"preesentation"** to ensure its (relevance) **relevancy** for my audience of (unit trust) **mutual fund,** (building society) **savings & loan association** and (property) **real estate** executives. Then I meet the (director) **vice-president** and perhaps the (chairman) **president** of the company organising the (conference) **convention...** Etc. *Get the picture?*

Considering there aren't that many countries in the world using English as their first language, the variation in proper terminology (not to mention slang) from one country to the next is as confusing as it is vast. Of course, the Americans' leadership in IT has meant that quite a few of their terms are now creeping into English as spoken elsewhere, mainly via the internet. Also, there are various resources on the internet which share terminology and jargon focusing on one geographical/ cultural or another.

But few of those resources give understandable comparisons, and the vocabulary of Silicon Valley doesn't cover the rest of life. That's why I have put this book together: over 2,000 of the most commonly used terms – including slang – from business jargon to different cuts of meat ... translated across the Atlantic and beyond.

Also, you'll find words and phrases specifically from regions of the United States and Canada; from southern

England, northern England, Scotland, Wales and Ireland; and from Australia and New Zealand. (NB: other than incidentally I haven't touched on the differences between US and British spellings ... that's for another book!)

If you think of more terms that should be in here (and I know there must be thousands,) please let me have them for the next edition, and I'll credit you on the acknowledgements page with a URL link to your business if appropriate.

Suze
Website: http://HowToWriteBetter.net
Email: suze@suzanstmaur.com

BRITISH
(AND BRITISH-RELATED)
ENGLISH

to North American English

A

A&E / Casualty
Emergency Room

A levels exams taken in 13th year of school, passes required for university entrance (England, Wales, Northern Ireland)

AS levels exams taken in the 12th year of school (England, Wales, Northern Ireland)

abattoir slaughterhouse

Aberdonian someone from Aberdeen, Scotland

abroad overseas

abseil rappel

accelerator gas pedal

accommodation accommodations

accident/crash (car) car wreck

advocate (Scotland) attorney, barrister

aerial (radio/TV) antenna (both used everywhere)

afore (Scotland) before

Aga (brand name) popular cooking stove/range

air gun BB gun

aisle gangway

alarm call wakeup call

Alsation German Shepherd dog (also called German Shepherd)

alternative alternate (adj.), also alternative

aluminium aluminum

amber fluid (Australia, NZ) beer

amber light (traffic lights) yellow light

ambo (Australia, NZ) ambulance

American football football

American Indians (people) Indians/First Nation

anaesthetist anesthesiologist

angry mad

angry pissed

anorak parka

Annual General Meeting (AGM) Annual Stockholders' Meeting

antenatal prenatal

anticlockwise counterclockwise

any road (northern England) anyway

around the bend/twist mentally challenged

arse ass

arseholed drunk

Articles of Association bylaws

articulated lorry/artic trailer truck, transport

arvo (Australia, NZ) afternoon

Asians (people) east Indians

assistant, shop assistant clerk, sales clerk

athletics (sport) track and field

at a pinch if absolutely necessary

at a rate of knots very fast

at the weekend on the weekend

aubergine egg plant

auld (Scotland) old

Auld Reekie (Scotland) Edinburgh

auspiced (adj.) (Australia) something under the auspices of...

Australian Taxation Office equivalent to HMRC

authorised share capital authorized capital stock

autumn fall

autocue teleprompter

avocado, avocado pear alligator pear

aye yes – Scotland, northern Ireland, Republic of Ireland, northern England

B

baggage luggage

bags I / bagsie keep for me (e.g. "bagsie that cupcake)

bairn (Scotland) baby, child

balaclava woolen head and neck covering with holes for eyes and nose

bang on, nag harp (v.)

banger sausage, also old, worn-out car

bank holiday national/public/legal holiday

bank note bill

bap bun, hamburger bun

barbie (Australia, NZ) barbecue

barking (adj.) lunatic, crazy

barman/barmaid bartender/barkeeper

barmy crazy

barney (n.) fight

barometer stock bellweather stock

barrister trial lawyer

base rate (finance) prime rate

bash (n.) party (n.)

basin (wash or hand) sink

basket (laundry) hamper

bat (ping pong, table tennis) paddle

bath (n.) bathtub

bath (v.) bathe

bathroom bathroom/restroom/washroom

battery accumulator (also called battery)

be sick (vomit) throw up

beastie (Scotland) insect, bug

beaut (Australia, NZ) good, great, pretty, etc.

bed & breakfast rate (hotel) European plan

bedside table nightstand

bedsit bed-sitting room – efficiency apartment

beefburger hamburger

beetroot beet/beets

ben (Scottish) mountain

bend/corner (road) curve/turn

benefits welfare

bent crooked, dishonest

bespoke tailor made

bevvy (Scottish) drink, usually alcoholic

bicarbonate of soda baking soda

big dipper roller coaster

big girl's blouse weakling, coward

bill (v.) charge

bill (n.) check

bill, the police

billabong (Australia) an oxbow lake

billiards game similar to pool

billion = 1million million billion = 1 thousand million (US version now widely used in UK)

billy (Australia) kettle, tea kettle

bin liner garbage bag

bird girl, chick

biro ballpoint pen

biscuit (sweet) cookie

biscuit/cracker (unsweetened) cracker

biscuit tin, barrel cookie jar

black cab purpose built so-called "London taxi" seen in most UK cities

black or white? (coffee) with cream or without?

black pudding blood sausage

blackleg/scab scab (person who won't conform to union)

black treacle molasses

bladdered drunk

blag steal, cadge

blank (v.) ignore

blether (Scotland) talk, chatter

Blighty former term for Britain, from Hindustani

blimey expression of surprise, probably from "Bless Me"

blind (window) shade (both terms widely used)

block of flats apartment building

bloke guy, man

bloomer blooper, mistake

blotto drunk

blow me! I am surprised!

blub to cry

blue (Australia) fight (n.), mistake

Bob's your uncle there you go – problem solved

boffin technical expert, scientist, etc.

bog marsh, wetland

bog toilet, lavatory

boiler (heating) furnace

bolshie/bolshy (n. and adj.) (Bolshevik) rebellious type

bonnet (car) hood

bonnie (Scotland) pretty, beautiful

bonus / capitalization issue stock dividend / stock split

bonzer (Australia) good, great

book (v.) make reservation

bookstall newsstand

boot (car) trunk

Borstal reform school

botch/bodge (v. and adj.) careless repair or fixing

bottom drawer (bride to be) hope chest

bottle courage

bouncy castle (children's amusement) bounce house

bowler hat derby hat

box junction intersection where no-one can stop inside the marked lines, to prevent jams

boycott ban, ostracize

boyo (endearment) (male) pal, friend, used in Wales

braces (to hold up trousers) suspenders

brackets (writing) parentheses

brae (Scotand) slope, hillside

braising steak chuck steak, blade roast

brass money (northern England)

brassed off annoyed, fed up

break (school) recess

break up, to (school) to end school term and start vacation

bridging loan bridge loan

bridie (Scotland) small meat pie, pasty

briefs/underpants shorts, jockey shorts

bring a plate (Australia, NZ) bring some food to share

broad bean lima bean

brogue strong accent, especially Irish, also style of shoe

brook, stream creek, stream (small rivers)

browned off fed up

bubble and squeak dish made from fried leftover potatoes, cabbage and other vegetables

bucket pail

bucks fizz (drink) mimosa

buggy (golf) cart

bully for you good for you, aren't you clever

builder construction worker, or construction company owner

building industry construction industry

building society savings & loan association

bum (backside) butt, fanny

bum bag fanny pack

bumf paperwork, promotional literature, instructions, etc.

bumper (car) fender (fender can also mean car body wing)

bung (v.) throw, also slang for bribe (n. and v.)

bureau de change currency exchange

burgle burglarize

burn (n.) (Scotland) stream, very small river

busybody buttinski

buttocks fanny, bum, buns

butty sandwich

C

CID (Criminal Investigation Department) plain clothes police detectives

CV (curriculum vitae) résumé

cactus (Australia) (adj.) not functioning, dead

call box phone booth

candyfloss cotton candy

cannae (Scotland) cannot

canny (Scotland) clever, cunning

canteen cafeteria

camper van RV (recreational vehicle), motorhome

caravan trailer, mobile home

caravan site trailer park

caretaker/porter janitor

carnival parade

car boot, car boot sale similar to garage or yard sale but held out of trunks of cars on land rented for the purpose

car park parking lot

carriage (train) car

carryout (Scottish, fast food) take out, to go

carsey toilet, washroom

cash dispenser ATM (automated teller machine)

cashier (bank) teller

cashpoint machine ATM (automated teller machine)

castor sugar super fine sugar

catapult sling shot

cattle grid Texas gate, cattle guard

ceilidh (pro. kaylee) Gaelic for party, concert, dance

cellar basement

central reservation (road) median

centre (city/business) downtown

chairman (business) president

chambers lawyers' offices

chat up, to sweet-talk, hit on

chav hillbilly, hoodlum

cheeky naughty, lively

cheerio goodbye, so long

cheers thank you, also here's to your good health

cheesed off fed up, mildly angry

chemist/pharmacist druggist

chemist's shop/pharmacy drugstore

chest of drawers bureau

chestnut (horses, colour) sorrel

chicory Belgian endive

Chinese burn Indian burn

chinless refers to British upper class, assuming many have receding chins, also moral weakness

chinless wonder person as described above!

chintzy like old-fashioned floral upholstery

chipolata slimmer version of classic British sausage

chips French fries/fries

chippy fish and chip stall, also carpenter/wood worker

chocablock, chockers choc full

Christian/given name first name

chrysanthemums mums

chuck throw

chuffed pleased

chunder (Australia, NZ) vomit, throw up

cinema, "the pictures" movie theater, movie house

city centre, town centre downtown

clachan (Scotland) village, very small town

clacker (Australia) anus

clanger, to drop a to make a tactless mistake

clapped out worn out (e.g. car)

class/form/year (school) grade

Claymore (Scotland) large sword

clingfilm plastic wrap/saran wrap (Saran is a brand name in USA)

clipped (e.g. horse, dog, etc.) shaved

cloakroom checkroom

clobber (n.) clothes, clothing

clobber (v.) hit, smack, assault

clock (v.) notice, take note of, observe

close (n.) dead-end street, usually small and suburban

cloth rag

coach (vehicle) bus

cobblers nonsense

cock-a-leekie (Scotland) chicken and leek soup

cockerel rooster

Cockney Rhyming Slang words or phrases that rhyme with the word to be substituted, e.g. "barnet fair" instead of "hair. Originates from London. There are numerous Cockney Rhyming Slang resources on the internet – Google shows over 300,000 – but one of my favourites is http://www.aldertons .com/english-.htm.

cocktail stick toothpick (also called toothpick in UK)

codswallop nonsense

coffin casket

coloured (horses) paint (i.e. horses coloured white plus one or two other colours)

college (mostly) alternative to university, tends to be more vocationally orientated

commissioner for oaths notary public

competence competency

complaint, complain beef (n. and v.)

complete (v., property) close

concrete (substance) cement (incorrect but used, esp. Canada)

conference convention

consultant (medical) specialist (medical)

Continent, The how older Brits refer to mainland Europe

continental breakfast breakfast as more usual in mainland Europe, e.g. bread, buns, fruit, etc.

contraceptive/condom rubber (may be confused with UK "eraser")

cooked breakfast English breakfast, e.g. bacon, sausage, eggs, tomato, black pudding, toast, etc.

cooker stove/range

cookery book cookbook

coriander cilantro

corn flour corn starch

corporation/local authority municipal government

cos lettuce romaine lettuce

cot (for baby) crib

Cottage Pie oven-baked dish of hamburger meat (beef) in gravy topped with mashed potato

cotton (in sewing) thread

cotton reel spool of thread

cotton wool cotton batting ("Cotton wool" widely understood in USA)

couch grass crab grass

council (n.) (local government) municipal government

council house, flat, estate municipality-owned subdivision, rented apartment, rented house

courgette zucchini

court shoe pump

cover / insurance cover insurance

craic (Irish) (pron. "crack") fun, good time

cream cracker soda cracker

crèche day nursery or day care center

credit card charge card

creditors accounts payable

crikey! goodness me!

Crimbo, Crimble childish name for Christmas

crime, criminal felony, felon

crisps chips, potato chips

croft (Scotland) small farm, smallholding

crofter (Scotland) owner or tenant of small farm or smallholding

crook (adj.) (Australia) unwell, not feeling right

crossroads intersection

crumble rich fruit pie rather like cobbler

crumpet small cake eaten hot with butter, jam, etc

crutch crotch

cul-de-sac dead end

cupboard closet

current account (bank) checking account

curtains drapes

Cumberland Pie oven-baked dish of hamburger meat (beef) in gravy mixed with diced carrots or other cooked vegetables, topped with mashed potato

Cumberland sausages very long sausages traditionally coiled for cooking and serving

curtains drapes

cutlery silverware/flatware

D

daft stupid

Dáil Éireann lower house of parliament, Republic of Ireland

dear (adj.) expensive

debtors accounts receivable

dekko, take a take a look

demolish (building) tear down

desiccated (coconut) shredded

diary (business) calendar

diddicoy (slang) gypsy of mixed Romany and other, often Irish, culture

digestive biscuits popular cookies made with whole wheat flour and wheat germ

dinkum (Australia) genuine, real

dinnae (Scotland) do not

dinner jacket tuxedo

director (company) vice president

directory enquiries "information"

disembark (from aircraft) deplane

dish cloth dish rag

district precinct

("district" can be used everywhere)

diversion (on road) detour

doddle something that's very easy to do

dodgy untrustworthy, potentially unsafe

dole unemployment benefit (welfare)

donger (Australia) penis

donkey's years a very long time

dosh money

Downs upland areas in south-east England

double cream heavy cream

drain (indoors) sewer pipe

dram (Scotland) shot of (Scotch) whisky

draughts (board game) checkers

drawing pin thumb tack

dress circle (theatre) mezzanine

dressing-gown bathrobe/robe (both terms can be used everywhere)

drive name-type of small suburban street, also driveway

driving licence driver's license

drunk driver impaired driver

dual carriageway divided/4 lane highway

duchess (Australia) buffet, sideboard

duck (endearment) dear (midlands of England)

dumb unable to speak

dummy (baby) pacifier

dungarees overalls (both terms can be used everywhere)

dust cart garbage truck

dustbin/bin garbage/trash can

duster dust rag

dustman garbage collector

dyke, dike bank to prevent watercourse from flooding, levee – also (offensive) lesbian

E

earth (v.) (electricity) ground

earth (soil) dirt

eat humble pie eat crow

economy class (air travel) coach

Edinburgh Trades (Scotland) first 2 weeks of July in Edin. when some businesses close for vacation

eejit (Scotland) idiot

eggy bread (food) French toast

eiderdown comforter/quilt

elastic band rubber band

electricity supply hydro (most of Canada where electricity is generated by water movement)

Emergency telephone numbers
999 (UK & Rep. of Ireland)
112 (UK, Rep. of Ireland, all other EC)
911 (USA & Canada)
000 (Australia)
111(New Zealand)
112 (South Africa)

emulsion paint latex paint

engaged (phone) busy

engine (car) motor

English breakfast
usually eggs, bacon, sausage, tomatoes, mushrooms, sometimes baked beans and black pudding, plus toast, jam or marmalade and beverages

envisage envision

escape road (motoring) runaway ramp

esky (Australia) cooler, cool box)

estate agent realtor, real estate broker

estate car station wagon

ex-directory unlisted (phone numbers)

expiry expiration

F

4WD/off-roader
(vehicle) SUV (sports
utility vehicle)

factotum gofer, runner,
someone who is at your
beck and call

fag cigarette

faggots type of
meatballs served in gravy

fair/funfair carnival

fancy (v.) desire (v.)

fanny vulva

fête fair, usually rural

Fianna Fáil political
party, Republic of Ireland

fill out (e.g. details) fill in

fillet steak filet
mignon/steak tenderloin

**filling station / petrol
station** gas station
(filling station works
everywhere)

film (n.) movie, motion
picture

Fine Gael political party,
Republic of Ireland

finished, (e.g.) I have
done (e.g.) I am

finished, (e.g.) I have
through (e.g.) I'm

fire, electric or gas space
heater

fire brigade fire department

fire engine fire truck

first floor second floor

firth (Scotland) estuary

fish fingers fish sticks

fitted carpet wall-to-wall carpet, broadloom

fizzy drink (non-alcoholic) pop (Canada) soda (USA)

flannel (washing) facecloth, washcloth

flat (home, owned) condo, condominium

flat (rented) apartment

flat mate room mate

flex electric cord/cable

flunky (Scotland) servant

fly-over overpass

food shopping grocery shopping, groceries

football/soccer soccer

footpath, bridleway trail (bridleway is for horses)

fortnight two weeks

foyer lobby

frankfurter (food) weiner

freephone toll free

fringe (hair) bangs

frock dress (n.)

fruit machine slot machine

frying pan skillet

full board (hotel)
American plan

full stop (punctuation)
period

funeral director
mortician

G

GCSE (General Certificate of Secondary Education) exams taken in the 11th year of school (England, Wales, Northern Ireland)

gaff (from French gaffe) mistake, boo-boo

gaff (slang) home, house or apartment

gaffer boss, also electrician

gaffer tape electrical or insulation tape, similar to duct tape

gallery (theatre) balcony

gallivant fool around, socialize (usually derogatory)

gammy lame, injured, e.g. "gammy leg"

gaol (prison) jail, penitentiary

garage (car servicing) workshop/shop

Garda police force in the Republic of Ireland

garden (n.) yard, back yard

gazump (property/real estate) when a money offer for a house of other property, having been accepted by the owner, is subsequently exceeded and accepted by the owner thereby bypassing the previous offerer – illegal in Scotland

gearbox transmission

gear lever gear shift

geek technical enthusiast

geezer man, guy, fellow

general practitioner (GP) family doctor, primary care doctor

Geordie person from the Newcastle area of north-east England

Gents men's room

get dressed dress (v.)

giddy dizzy (both terms widely used)

gilt-edge stock (gilts) Treasury bonds

ginger hair red hair

git idiot

give a bell (to phone) call, give a buzz

give way (motoring) yield

Glasgow Fair (Scotland) 3rd and 4th weeks of July, when some businesses close for vacation

glen (Scotland) deep valley

gloaming (Scotland) dusk, sundown

glove box (car) glove compartment

gob mouth, yap

golden syrup similar to light treacle or maple syrup

golf buggy golf cart

goods train freight train

goods truck freight truck

goolies testicles

goose pimples goose bumps

got gotten

grease-proof paper wax paper

greasy spoon (food) local diner, esp. cheap type

green fingers green thumb (means someone is good at growing plants)

greengrocer person/business selling fruit and vegetables

grill (v.) broil

grill (n.) broiler

grockle rather snotty word for lower-class person

grog (Australia,NZ) liquor, beer, booze

grotty disgusting, pathetic, poor

ground floor first floor/street level

grub food, "chow"

guard (railway) conductor

guard's van caboose, but on passenger trains as well as freight trains

guide dog seeing eye dog

gumboots rubber boots, wellington boots

gun dog bird dog

gutter (building) eaves trough

gym shoes/plimsolls/tennis shoes/trainers running shoes/sneakers

gyppy tummy stomach upset, diarrhea

H

HMRC (Her Majesty's Revenue and Customs) US equivalent is IRS (Internal Revenue Service)

haggis (Scotland) type of spherical sausage filled with meat, oatmeal, herbs etc.

hair grip/kirby grip bobby pin

hair lacquer hair spray

hair slide barrette

hairpin bend switchback

handbag purse

handbrake (car) parking brake

hard core construction and other rubble used as foundation fill, also heavy-duty e.g. "hardcore porn"

hard shoulder (road) shoulder

harp (n.) musical instrument – as verb, not used in UK

hash key number key

head master/mistress/teacher principal

head waiter maître d, maître d'hotel

hen/stag night bachelorette/bachelor night

hessian (fabric) burlap

hiccough hiccup

high tea meal eaten in early evening, also dinner, supper, tea

hire rent

hire car rental car

hire purchase installment plan

Highers/Advanced Highers exams taken by pupils in their final years of secondary education (Scotland only)

hoarding billboard

hob element/ring (cooker) burner

hockey field hockey

Hogmany (Scotland) New Year's Eve

holiday vacation, holidays

holiday maker vacationer

Home Counties counties in south-east England which border on London

hooligan badly behaved person, usually young, vandal

Hooray Henry loud-mouthed, rather silly upper class British man

hoose (Scotland) house, home

hoover (n.) vacuum cleaner (Hoover is brand name, used in UK)

hoover (v.) vacuum (clean)

house train (pets) housebreak

housing estate sub-division

housewife homemaker

hump, to have the to be angry or offended

hunting (sport) fox hunting

I

Ibuprofen Advil (Advil is a widely-used brand name) / ibuprofen

ice/sorbet sherbet

ice hockey hockey

iced lolly popsicle

icing (food) frosting

icing sugar powdered/confectioner's sugar

immersion heater (electric) water heater

in hospital in the hospital

indicators (car) turn lights

inglenook type of antique fireplace built so it forms a very small half-room off a main room

inheritance tax death tax

Inland Revenue New Zealand equivalent to HMRC

innit contraction of "isn't it?" (London and south-east England)

insult, criticize slate

interval (theatre) intermission

int-it contraction of "isn't it?" (northern England)

inverted commas (punctuation) quotation marks

invoice bill

Irish Stew slow-cooked dish made from fresh lamb, potatoes, onions and other vegetables

ironmongery, ironmonger hardware, hardware store

isnae (Scotland) is not

J

jab (injection) shot

jacket potato baked potato

jaffa cakes cookies filled with an orange-flavored jelly

jammy lucky

jelly (sweet) jello (Jello is a brand name in US – Jell-O)

jetski sea-doo (Canada)

jobsworth intransigent person who won't overstep rules to help you ("more than my job's worth")

"Joe Bloggs" "John Doe"

joiner experienced and skilled carpenter

joint (meat) roast

jug pitcher

juggernaut 18-wheeler/trailer truck/transport

jersey (clothing) sweater

jumble sale rummage sale

jumper/sweater/pullover sweater

jump rope skipping rope

K

kebab kabob

kedgeree old-fashioned breakfast or supper dish of rice, smoked fish, hard-boiled eggs, herbs and flavorings

ken (Scotland) know, e.g. "do you ken him?"

khazi toilet

kibosh, kybosh end, finish, e.g. "put the kibosh on it"

kiosk/box (telephone) phone booth

kip (n.) nap, short sleep

kipper (food) smoked herring

kirk (Scotand) church

kitchen paper/roll paper towels

Kiwi (slang) person from New Zealand

knackered worn out

knees-up party, celebration

knickers (girl's) panties

knock up (tennis) warm up

knock up (call from sleep) wakeup call ("Knock up" also can mean get a woman pregnant, all English speakers)

know-it-all wise guy, smart ass, know-all

L

L plates signs on front and rear of learner driver's car

ladder (tights) run (pantyhose)

ladies' toilet powder room

ladybird (insect) ladybug

lag (v.) to insulate e.g. roof, pipes, water tanks etc.

laird (Scotland) lord, landlord

Lancashire Hotpot oven-baked dish of lamb and vegetables topped with sliced potato

land (property/real estate) ground

landline house phone

lang (Scotland) long

lang syne (Scotland) long ago

larder pantry

launderette laundromat

lavatory/toilet/w.c./ loo bathroom/washroom/ restroom

lay the table set the table

lay-by pull-off, turn-out

lead (n.) (dog) leash

lemon curd sweet spread made from lemon juice, sugar, butter and eggs, also made with orange

lemonade soda/pop drink like 7-Up

lemonade (home made) similar to North American home made lemonade

let (v.) rent (as in homes/property)

level crossing (railway) grade crossing

lie in (sleep late) sleep in

lift elevator

lightning conductor lightning rod

limited (company) incorporated company

liver sausage liverwort

loan (n., Scotland) lane, very small, narrow street

local authority (also council) municipal government

loch (Scotland) lake

lodger boarder, roomer

loft attic

log book the "V5" form that shows details of a car or other small motor vehicle's "registered keeper"

loo toilet/washroom/ bathroom/washroom

lollypop lady/man crossing guard (e.g. outside school)

lorry truck

lorry park truck stop

lost property lost and found

love bite hickey

lugs ears

lum (Scotland) chimney

lunch box lunch pail

lunge (horses) longe

mackintosh/mac
raincoat

mad insane, crazy

made to measure
custom made

magistrate municipal
judge

mains household or
other plug-in electrical
supply, as opposed to
battery power

mains general term
describing individual
utilities systems

managing director/MD
general manager (varies
according to nature of
company)

Mancunian someone
from Manchester,
England

mangetout snow peas

manual (car gears)
standard/stick shift

marrow (vegetable)
squash

mash mashed potatoes

mate buddy (friend)

maths math

mean stingy/tightwad

**Memorandum of
Association** Certificate
of Incorporation

mend/repair/renovate
fix/fix up

merchant bank
investment bank

mess about fool around

messages (Scotland)
shopping (n.)

mews little street in pre-20th century urban areas, normally behind a much grander street or avenue, where the old stables and servants' quarters have been converted into bijou "mews houses"

mileometer odometer (both terms widely used)

MILITARY: BRITISH AIR FORCE RANKS
(Canada, Australia and New Zealand are similar)
Aircraftman
Leading Aircraftman
Senior Aircraftman

Junior Technician
Corporal
Sergeant
Chief Technician
Flight-Sergeant
Warrant Officer
Pilot Officer
Flying Officer
Flight-Lieutenant
Squadron Leader
Wing Commander
Group Captain
Air Commodore
Air Vice-Marshal
Air Marshal
Air Chief Marshal
Marshal of the Royal Air Force

MILITARY: BRITISH ARMY RANKS
(Canada, Australia and NZ are similar)
Private
Lance Corporal
Corporal
Sergeant
Staff/Colour Sergeant
Warrant Officer Class 2
(Company/Squadron

Sergeant Major)
Warrant Officer Class 1
(Regimental Sergeant
Major)
Officer Cadet
Second Lieutenant
Lieutenant
Captain
Major
Lieutenant Colonel
Colonel
Brigadier
Major General
Lieutenant General
General

MILITARY: BRITISH NAVY RANKS

(Canada, Australia and
New Zealand are similar)
Rating
Leading Hand
Petty Officer
Chief Petty Officer
Warrant Officer
Acting Sublieutenant
Sublieutenant
Lieutenant
Lieutenant-Commander

Commander
Captain
Commodore
Rear Admiral
Vice Admiral
Admiral
Admiral of the Fleet

mince (food) ground
beef/pork/etc / hamburger

minger/mingin
originally a Scottish word
for dirty/smelly/horrible
thing or person

minicab ordinary sedan
or MPV used as taxi, as
opposed to "black cab"

mobile phone mobile
cellphone

momentarily for a brief
moment

monkey southern UK
slang for GBP £500

motorway freeway, highway, multi-lane highway, expressway

motorway services service station

muck about pretend, fool around

muesli breakfast cereal like granola, except ingredients are raw

multi-storey car park parking garage

mum mom (short forms for "mother")

music hall (entertainment) vaudeville

music notes:
breve double whole note
semibreve whole note
minim half note
crotchet quarter note
quaver eighth note
semiquaver sixteenth note
demisemiquaver thirty-second note

muslin cheese cloth

N

naff (adj) inferior

nag, bang on harp (v.)

nail varnish, nail lacquer nail polish

nappy diaper

national insurance number social security number

nauseated nauseous

neat (drink) straight

neap (Scotland) turnip

nerd dork, person with no social skills

net curtains sheers

newsagent like a newsstand but a larger store selling candy, cigarettes, a few convenience products

naught/nought zero

naughts/noughts and crosses tic-tac-toe

naughty bits genitals

nick (n.) prison, police custody

nick (v.) arrest by police

nick (v.) to steal

no claims bonus good driver discount

nonsense baloney (slang)

normality normalcy

nosey parker busybody, nosy person

nosh (n. and v.) food, to eat

nosh-up good meal

note (money) bill

number plate (car) license plate

OAP (Old Age Pensioner) senior citizen

off licence/wine merchant liquor store

offal organ meat

office block office building

old bill police

old car jalopy

on heat in heat

on the blink broken

on the job can mean having sex

one-to-one one-on-one

optician (dispensing) optician

optician (ophthalmic) optometrist

ordinary share common stock

Orientals (people) Asians

orientate orient

outback (Australia) bush, wild countryside

outside lane (4+ lane highway) inside lane

oven cloth/gloves oven mitt, pot holder

overalls coveralls

overheads overhead

overtake (vehicle) pass

P

P&P (postage & packaging) S&H (shipping & handling)

pack (of cards) deck

packed lunch brown bag lunch

packet (sweets etc) pack

Paddy English term for someone from the Republic of Ireland

palaver (n.) fuss, bother

panda car local police car so called due its white and colored paint job

pantomime light theater production usually in winter holiday season, aimed at young families

pants (boy's underwear) shorts/underwear

paracetamol acetaminophen, Tylenol (brand name)

parade of shops strip mall

paraffin (liquid) kerosene

paraffin (wax) paraffin

parcel package

pastie small meat pie

pavement/footpath
sidewalk

pear-shaped description
of something that has
gone wrong

pedestrian crossing
crosswalk

peebo (child's game)
peekaboo

pensioner senior citizen,
senior

perspex Plexiglass

people carrier (vehicle)
MPV (multi-purpose
vehicle) / van

pepper/coffee mill
pepper/coffee grinder

period menstrual period

personal call person-to-
person call

pet (endearment) dear
(north-east England)

petrol gasoline/gas

petrol station gas
station

physiotherapy physical
therapy

physiotherapist
physical therapist

photocopier (machine)
Xerox (brand name)

picture rail real estate –
molding in older-style
rooms about 12 inches
from ceiling, from which
picture frames could be
hung

pickaxe pick

piece of cake something
that's easy to do

pigsty pig pen

pigtails braids

pikelet also crumpet, small cake eaten hot with butter, jam, etc

pikey (offensive) term used derogatively to describe Travellers, Roma Gypsies, etc

pillar box/letter box/post box mail box

pillock, prat idiot, dumb-ass

pinch, nick steal

pished (Scotland) drunk (adj.)

piss artist drunkard

pissed drunk

pissed off angry, fed up

plait (n. and v.) braid (n. and v.)

plant (n.) equipment used in construction process

plaster/Elastoplast (brand name) Bandaid (brand name)

play gooseberry be unwanted 3rd party on date

pleb yokel, hick

plonk cheap wine

plot (of land) lot

Ploughman's lunch popular "pub" plate of cheese, bread and strong pickles

pneumatic drill jackhammer

point/power point/socket outlet/socket

polis (Scotland) the Police

polo neck (sweater) turtle neck

polo shirt golf shirt

pom, pommie (Australia) (offensive) English person

ponce (n.) one who lives off earnings of prostitutes, also freeloader

ponce (v.) to freeload off someone

pontoon card game like 21 or blackjack

poorly sick(unwell)

pork scratchings (food) pork rinds

posh upper class, upscale

post (n. & v.) mail (n. & v.)

post code zip code (USA) postal code (Canada)

postman mailman

postponement raincheck

poteen (Irish) illegally made liquor, similar to "moonshine"

potter (v.) to putter, e.g. around back yard

power cut power outage

pram baby carriage/buggy

prawn shrimp

prefect (school) monitor

prep school private school (primary/public school level)

presently soon

prison penitentiary

prize draw prize drawing (competition, contest etc)

profit and loss account income statement

property (housing etc) real estate

public convenience restroom available to public, not always for free!

public school private school (high school level)

pudding/sweet dessert

pukka genuine, correct (from Hindi)

puncture (car tyre) flat, flat tire

punter horse racing better, but also customer, client

purse change purse, pocket book

pushchair stroller

put through (telephone) connect

quarrel argument

quarter to quarter of
(time, 15 minutes before
hour)

quay dock

queue (n.) line/line-up

queue (v.) line up/stand
in line

quid UK money, one
pound

quite absolutely, you're
right

quoted company listed
company

R

railway railroad

railway engine locomotive

rambler hiker

randy sexually aroused, horny

rapeseed oil canola

rasher (bacon) slice

rather, (e.g.) I would sooner, (e.g.) I would

Rawlplug (brand name UK) screw anchor

reception (hotel) front desk

receptionist front desk clerk

redundant, made redundant (employment) laid off

reek (Scotland) (n. and v.) smoke (n. and v.)

registration plate (car) license plate

relevance relevancy

rellies (mostly Australia, NZ) relatives

removals moving (house)

renovate remodel (e.g. house, kitchen)

retail price index consumer price index

return ticket round trip ticket

reverse charges (phone) collect

reverse (v.) (driving) back up

revise study (e.g. for examinations)

ring, ring up (v.) (phone) call (phone)

ring off (phone) hang up

ring road beltway around town or city

ripper (Australia) (adj.) excellent, very good

rise (in pay) raise

Riviera, the French older Brits use this to name the Mediterranean coast in south-eastern France, roughly from Cannes in the west to Menton in the east and crossing the border into Italy to San Remo (where of course it becomes the Italian Riviera.) Was a popular area for rich Brits to spend the winter up to around the mid 20th century.

road surface pavement

roadworks (road sign) (highway) construction

rockery rock garden

rocket (salad) arugula

roll (bread) bun

roof/hood (car) top

roof rack (car) luggage rack

rooftiles (building) shingles

round (n.) session or activity, e.g. round of drinks in a bar, round of government talks

roundabout (road) traffic circle, rotary

row (n. and v.) (pron. rah-oo) fight (n. and v.) (argument)

rubber eraser (NOT contraceptive!)

rubbish (n.) garbage, also nonsense

rubbish (v.) to denigrate, criticize

rump steak sirloin steak

runner beans string beans

S

sack, get the fired, get

saloon (car) sedan

sand pit sand box

sanger (Australia) sandwich

sarnie (UK) sandwich

Sassenach (Scotland) English person (slightly derogatory)

savoury roll (bread) biscuit, bun

scribbling pad/block scratch pad

Scotch (England) Scotch whisky, but must never be used to mean "Scottish!"

scouse, scouser someone from Liverpool, England

Seanad Éireann upper house of parliament, Republic of Ireland

secateurs pruning shears

secondary glazing storm windows

seaside the beach

see-saw teeter-totter

Sellotape Scotch tape (both are brand names)

semi-detached (house) duplex

semolina cream of wheat

service flats apartment hotel

share (n.) stock

share premium paid-in surplus

shareholder stockholder

shareholders' equity stockholders' equity

shattered exhausted

sheila (Australia) girl, woman

Shepherd's Pie oven-baked dish of ground fresh or diced leftover lamb in gravy topped with mashed potatoes

shirty slightly aggressive, unpleasant in demeanor

shooting hunting (birds, etc.)

shop assistant sales clerk/counter clerk

shopping centre/precinct shopping mall

shopping trolley shopping cart

shouldnae (Scotland) should not

sick (n.) vomit (n.)

sick (current) excellent, very good

sick (previously) weird, in bad taste

sideboard buffet

sideboards (hair) sideburns

England, Wales and Northern Ireland

sidelights parking lights

skew whiff crooked, unlevel, visually distorted

silencer (car) muffler

skim milk skimmed milk

silver, solid silver, sterling (esp. Canada)

skint penniless, having no money

silverside (food, beef) top round

skip (n., rubbish container) dumpster

single ticket one-way ticket

skipping rope jump rope

Sinn Féin political party, Republic of Ireland

skirting board baseboard

sirloin steak porterhouse steak

slap up meal large, elaborate lunch or dinner

sitting room / living room / lounge / drawing room / front room living room

slate (v.) schedule (v.)

sledge, sleigh toboggan/sled

sixth form last 2 years of secondary education in

sliproad entry or exit ramp

smalls (washing) underwear

smashing good

smoked salmon lox

snog (v.) neck (v.), play tonsil hockey, heavy petting

snooker game similar to pool

snowmobile ski-doo (Canada)

snug/TV room family room/den

sofa/settee/couch couch/davenport

soda soda water

solicitor/barrister lawyer/attorney

sorbet sherbet

sorted done, accomplished

spanner wrench

spanner (adjustable) monkey wrench

sparrow fart dawn, very early morning

spend a penny use toilet

spirits (drink) liquor/hard liquor

spring onion green onion/scallion/salad onion

sprouts usually means Brussels sprouts

spunk semen

squiffy slightly drunk

stabilisers training wheels (for child's bicycle)

staff (n.) (academic) faculty

stalls (theatre) orchestra seats

stand (v.) (e.g. for public office) run

stands, grandstands bleachers

standard lamp floor lamp

stanley knife box cutter

starter (meal) appetizer

state school public school (primary) / high school (secondary)

station (Australia,NZ) large farm or area of grazing land

stay (Scotland) live, reside, as in "where do you stay?"

stewing steak flank steak

stickybeak (Australia) busybody, nosy person

stiffie formal invitation printed on hard (i.e. stiff) board

stock (business, retail) inventory

stock cube (food) bouillon cube

stone (fruit) pit

stop quit (e.g. quit/stop smoking)

strimmer (gardening) weed whacker

stroppy upset, angry, unwilling

struck off (e.g. lawyer) disbarred

study, read major in (main university subject)

stuffing (food) dressing

stupid person bonehead

subway underpass

sultana/raisin/currant raisin

supply teacher substitute teacher

sure certain

surgery (doctor's/dentist's) doctor's office/dentist's office

surgical spirit rubbing alcohol

surname last name

suspender belt garter belt

suspenders braces

swede rutabaga/Swedish turnip

sweet dessert

sweet corn corn

sweet potato yam

sweet shop/ confectioner candy store

sweets candy

swimming costume bathing suit

Swiss roll jelly roll

T

table (v.) to designate a topic for discussion now

tadpole pollywog/tadpole

tap faucet

take the piss tease, humiliate

takeaway (food) to go, take out

tarmac asphalt, blacktop

tartan plaid

tax disc round label that must be displayed on car windshield to show annual duty has been paid

tea room small café serving afternoon tea, maybe light lunches and other snacks too

tea towel dish towel

tea trolley tea cart

teat (baby's bottle) nipple

telegram wire (not used much these days!)

telephone box phone booth

telly television

term (academic) semester

terraced house townhouse

terraces (e.g. in stadium) bleachers

text (i.e. on phone) SMS

theatre (medical, operating) operating room (medical, OR)

theft larceny

tick check, as in tick/check the box

tick over (car engine) idle

tights pantyhose

timber (wood) lumber

time-table schedule

tin (container) can

tinnie (Australia) can, usually of beer

tip (n. and v.) dump, throw away

toastie toasted sandwich, usually with cheese plus ham, etc

toerag tramp, undesirable person

toffee (sweets) taffy

tombola a type of lottery usually done at small, rural fêtes

tonsillitis strep throat

torch flashlight

touch wood knock on wood (expression re: "for luck")

tow haul

towbar trailer hitch / tow hitch

trade union labor union

traffic lights traffic/stop lights/signals

tram (vehicle) street car

tramp (n.) bum, hobo

transport (n.) transportation, transit

transport café truck stop diner

travellers nomadic people, usually gypsies

treasure hunt (children's game) scavenger hunt

trilby (hat) fedora

trolley (shopping) cart

trousers pants

truncheon (police) nightstick

trunk call (phone) long distance

tube (Australia) can of drink, usually beer

tube/underground/metro subway

tucker (Australia) food

turn right/left make a right/left turn

turn-ups (trousers) cuffs

twitcher keen bird watcher

U

undergraduates:
1st year freshman
2nd year sophomore
3rd year junior
4th year senior

undertaker mortician,
funeral director

unit trust mutual fund

unkind mean

upmarket upscale

ute (Australia, NZ) small
pickup truck

V

vacuum flask / flask
Thermos (brand name)

valet (cars) detail, thorough clean inside and out

vest undershirt

vet/veterinary surgeon
vet/veterinarian

veteran vet/veteran

visible trade
merchandise trade

visit (n. and v.) act of going to see something, or the action of doing so, e.g. "visit a museum"

W. C. (water closet) toilet, lavatory, restroom, etc.

wain (Scotland) child

waistcoat vest

waiter/waitress server

wallet billfold / wallet

wally nerd, idiot, unintelligent person

wardrobe clothes closet

wash and iron launder

washing (n.) laundry

washing up (n. and v.) doing the dishes

wasp (insect) wasp/yellow jacket

waste disposal unit garburator (Canada)/garbage disposal unit

wasted drunk

wee (adj.) (Scotland) small

wee (n. and v.) urine, urinate

wellington boots galoshes, rubber boots, gumboots

wheel clamp (car) boot

whisky usually means Scotch whisky (also called "Scotch" in UK)

whiskey usually means Irish whiskey or refers to "American whiskey," i.e. bourbon

whole milk homogenized milk

windscreen (car) windshield

write off (v.) total (v., as in "total loss" – insurance)

write to write

XYZ

yob hillbilly, hoodlum

yokel pleb, hick

yonks a long time, e.g. "yonks ago"

zebra crossing pedestrian priority crosswalk shown by flashing orange lights and stripes across it

zed (letter Z) zee

Zimmer frame walker

zip zipper

NORTH AMERICAN ENGLISH

to British
(and British-related)
English

A

ATM (automated teller machine) cashpoint machine, also cash dispenser

à la mode a dessert dish – e.g. fruit pie – with a scoop of ice cream, usually vanilla flavored

acetaminophen, Tylenol (brand name) paracetamol

accommodations accommodation

accounts payable creditors

accounts receivable debtors

accumulator battery (battery also used in USA)

Advil (brand name) ibuprofen (generic) Nurofen (brand name)

air (v.) TV, radio, to be broadcast e.g. "this program airs Tuesday"

all way stop (Canada: **four-way stop**) intersection similar to a traffic roundabout, without the circle!

alligator pear avocado pear

allowance (children) pocket money

alternate (adj.)
alternative (usually –
"alternate" wrongly used
to mean "alternative")

aluminum aluminium

American plan (hotel)
full board

anesthesiologist
anaesthetist

angel food cake very
light and delicate sponge
cake

**Annual Stockholders'
Meeting** Annual General
Meeting (AGM)

antenna aerial
(radio/TV)

antsy nervous, impatient

anymore contraction of
"any more" now in
common use in UK as
well as USA

anyways anyway

apartment flat (rented)

apartment building
block of flats

apartment hotel service
flats

appetizer (meal) starter

applejack strong
alcoholic drink made
from distilled cider

arugula (salad) rocket

Asians (people)
Orientals

asphalt tarmac

ass arse, bum, backside

attic loft

**authorized capital
stock** authorized share
capital

B

BB gun air gun

BS short for bullshit

baby carriage/buggy pram

bachelorette/bachelor night hen/stag night

back up (driving) reverse

baked potato jacket potato

baking soda bicarbonate of soda

bandaid plaster/elastoplasts (Bandaid and Elastoplast are brand names)

balcony (theater) gallery

baloney nonsense, also (literal) bologna sausage

ballgame nearly always means baseball game

ballpark as above, baseball playing field

ballpoint pen biro (Biro is a brand name)

bangs (hair) fringe

barf (vomit) be sick

barrette hair slide

bartender/barkeeper barman/barmaid

baseboard skirting board

basement cellar

bath estate agent jargon: half bath (toilet and handbasin) three-quarter bath (that plus shower) and full (all that plus full bathtub)

bathe (v.) bath (v.)

bathing suit swimming costume

bathrobe/robe dressing-gown (both terms can be used everywhere)

bathroom/restroom/washroom bathroom/toilets

bathroom/restroom/washroom lavatory/toilet/w.c./loo

bathtub bath (n.)

Bay Area San Francisco Bay area, population roughly 7.5 million

bayou (southern USA) marshy, slow-moving watercourse

beach seaside (if on an ocean coast...)

Beantown Boston, MA

beat it! go away!

Beaver tail (Canada) oval pastry base with various toppings

bedroll less formalized version of a sleeping bag!

beef (n. and v.) complaint, complain

beemer BMW car

beet/beets beetroot

Belgian endive chicory

bellboy, bellhop porter in hotel

beltway ring road around town or city

bender prolonged session of drinking alcohol

bent angry

Bible Belt southern US states including the Carolinas, Georgia, Tennessee, Arkansas, Missouri, Oklahoma, Kansas

Big Apple, The New York City

Bid D, The Dallas, Texas

Big Easy, The New Orleans

Big Tomato, The Sacramento, state capital of California

bill (n.) bank note, also bill or invoice

billboard hoarding

billfold wallet

billion = 1 thousand million billion = 1million million (though US version now widely used in UK)

bird dog gun dog

biscuit savory roll (bread)

blacktop tarmac road surface

bleachers stands, grandstands, terraces

blood sausage black pudding

blooper bloomer, mistake

boarder lodger

boardwalk wooden walkway

bobby pin hair grip/kirby grip

bobby sox (old fashioned) girls' ankle socks

bogey man spooky imaginary stranger

bologna type of sausage similar to mortadella, often called "baloney"

bombed drunk

bonehead stupid person

boo-boo mistake

booby hatch old fashioned slang for psychiatric hospital or nursing home

boot (car) wheel clamp

bouillon cube (food) stock cube

bounce house (children's amusement) bouncy castle

boutonnière flowers worn in lapel buttonhole

box cutter stanley knife

braces suspenders

braid (n. and v.) plait (n. and v.)

braids pigtails

bridge loan bridging loan

broadloom fitted carpet

broil grill (v.)

broiler grill (n.)

broke, flat broke skint, having no money

brown bag lunch packed lunch

brownstone used to describe elegant older residential buildings, mostly in New York City

brunch late morning meal that combines breakfast and lunch

buck dollar, US, Canadian, Australian, New Zealand (South Africa – Rand)

buckeye horse chestnut tree

buddy mate

buffet sideboard

bull short for bullshit

bum, hobo tramp (n.)

bum steer disadvantageous deal, swindle (n.)

bummer disappointment

bun (bread) roll

bun, hamburger bun bap

bun buttock

bunch (n.) widely used to describe a largish number of almost anything

bureau chest of drawers

burglarize burgle

burlap (fabric) hessian

burner (stove) hob element

bus, Greyhound (vehicle) coach

busboy junior waiter in restaurant

busy (phonecall) engaged

butt arse, bum, backside

butt in to interfere with, intrude

butt out! go away and mind your own business!

buttinski busybody

buzz saw circular saw

Bylaws Articles of Association

Bytown Ottawa, Canada

C

caboose guard's van on goods train

cafeteria canteen

Cajun culture and people who came to North America from France, then to Nova Scotia etc., finally to Louisiana

calendar diary, wall calendar

call, give a buzz, phone give a bell/ring up/phone

camper shell caravan-type device which "clips" on to the back of a specially equipped pickup truck

can (container) tin

can slang for toilet

Canada Revenue Agency equivalent to HMRC

candy sweets

candy store sweet shop/confectioner

canola rapeseed oil

Canuck slang for Canadian person

Capitol equivalent to UK Houses of Parliament

car (train) carriage

car wreck accident/crash

cart (golf) buggy

cart (shopping) trolley

carnival fair/funfair

casket coffin

catsup another word for (tomato) ketchup

cell phone mobile phone

cement concrete

Certificate of Incorporation Memorandum of Association

change purse, **pocket book** purse

charge (v.) bill (v.)

charge card credit card

check (n.) bill (n.)

check (n.) tick, as in "check/tick the box"

checkroom cloakroom

checkers (game) draughts

checking account (bank) current account

cheese cloth muslin

chesterfield sofa, settee, couch, usually large

chew out tell off, scold

chintzy cheap

chipmunk small, very cute member of the squirrel family

chips, potato chips crisps

choc full chockablock, chockers

chow food, grub

chow down to eat

chowder substantial soup usually made from fish/seafood, potatoes and other vegetables

chuck steak, blade roast braising steak

cigarette fag (slang)

citation (law) summons

cilantro coriander

cinch, it's a easy

clam up stop discussing or talking

clerk, sales clerk assistant, shop assistant

clicks (Canada, Australia, NZ) kilometers

clip (v.) to cheat, swindle

clip joint seedy nightclub

close (v., real esate) complete

closet cupboard

clothes closet wardrobe

coach (air travel) economy class

cobbler rich fruit pie rather like UK crumble

collect (phonecall) reverse charges

comforter/quilt eiderdown

common stock (finance) ordinary share

community college tertiary education, alternative to university

competency competence

conceptualize conceive (e.g. creative work)

condo, condominium flat

conductor (railroad) guard

connect (phonecall) put through

construction (on road sign) roadworks

construction industry building industry

consumer price index retail price index

convention conference

conversate converse

cook out barbecue or other al fresco meal

cooler cool box

cookbook cookery book

cookie biscuit (sweet)

cookie jar biscuit tin, barrel

cops police

cord chopped firewood measure, usually 4' by 4' by 8'

corn bread semi-sweet bread made from corn flour

corn dog frankfurter dipped in batter (usually made from cornflour) then deep-fried

corn sweet corn

corn starch corn flour

cotton batting/wool cotton wool

cotton candy candyfloss

couch/davenport sofa/settee/couch

counterclockwise anticlockwise

coveralls overalls

Cowtown Calgary, Canada

cracker biscuit/cracker

crab grass couch grass

cream of wheat semolina

creek, stream brook, stream (also "burn," Scotland)

crib (for baby) cot

critter creature, often a furry animal

crosswalk pedestrian crossing

crossing guard (e.g. outside school) lollypop lady/man

crotch crutch

cube short for cubicle, as in open-plan office cubicle

cuffs (pants) turn-ups

currency exchange bureau de change

curve/turn (road) bend/corner

custom made made to measure

cut (v.) dilute, e.g. alcoholic drink

cut loose break free, let your hair down

D

davenport large couch, sofa bed

dead end cul-de-sac

death tax inheritance tax

deck (of cards) pack

den snug, TV room

deplane disembark from aircraft

derby hat bowler hat

desire (v.) fancy (v.)

dessert pudding/sweet/afters

detail (v., cars etc.) valet (v.)

detour (on highway) diversion

diaper nappy

diddly, diddly squat nothing

dig (v.) slightly old fashioned term for appreciate

diner roadside and/or transport café, fast food restaurant

dime ten cent coin

dirt (soil) earth

disbarred (e.g. lawyer) struck off

dishes/wash the dishes
do the washing up

dishrag dish cloth

dish towel tea towel

divided/4 lane highway
dual carriageway

dizzy giddy (both terms
widely used)

dock (n.) quay

**doctor's office/
dentist's office**
surgery(doctor's/dentist's)

doing the dishes
washing up

done (e.g.) I am
finished, (e.g.) I have

doohickey gadget

doorman porter,
security officer

dork nerd, person with
no social skills

downtown city centre

drapes curtains

dress (n.) frock (dress
also OK in UK)

dress (v.) get dressed

dressing (food, e.g.
turkey) stuffing

driver's license driving
licence

driveway drive

druggist
chemist/pharmacist

drugstore chemist's
shop/pharmacy

dumb stupid

dump (n. & v.) (garbage)
tip

dumpster (garbage etc.) **dust rag** duster
skip

duplex semi-detached,
house separated into two
units

E

East Coast states from Maine down to Washington DC, also called "Eastern Seaboard"

East Indians (people) Asians

eat crow eat humble pie

eaves trough (on building) guttering

efficiency apartment bedsit

egg plant aubergine

eighteen wheeler very large lorry

electric cord/cable flex

elevator lift

Emerald City Seattle, Washington State

Emergency Room A&E / Casualty

Emergency telephone numbers
  999 (UK & Rep. of Ireland)
  112 (UK, Rep. of Ireland and all other EC)
  911 (USA & Canada)
  000 (Australia)
  111(New Zealand)
  112 (South Africa)

entrée main course (restaurant)

entry or exit ramp (highway) sliproad

envision envisage

eraser rubber

escrow third party holding of all monies until deal is finalized

European plan (hotel) bed & breakfast rate

evidently apparently

expiration expiry

eye candy something pleasing to look at

F

facecloth, washcloth
flannel

faculty staff (academic)

fag (offensive)
homosexual

fall (season) autumn

**family doctor, primary
care doctor** general
practitioner (GP)

family room/den
snug/TV room

fanny buttocks, bum,
arse

fanny pack bum bag

faucet tap

fedora (hat) trilby

felony, felon crime,
criminal

fender (car) bumper or
body wing

fender bender small car
accident with minor
damage

field hockey hockey

fight (n. and v.) row (n.
and v.)

**filet mignon/steak
tenderloin** fillet steak

fill in (e.g. details) fill out

fire department fire
brigade

fire truck fire engine

fired, get sack, get the

first floor/street level ground floor

first name Christian/given name

First Nation American Indians

fish sticks fish fingers

fix mend/repair

fixer-upper slang for dilapidated house that needs renovation

flake, flaky undesirable person, someone/something answering that description

flank steak stewing steak

flashlight torch

flat/flat tire puncture

flip, flip out lose temper or control

floor lamp standard lamp

flunk fail

folks family

fool around mess about, muck about

football American football

four way stop (mostly Canada) similar to a traffic roundabout, without the circle!

fox hunting hunting (sport)

freeload to "ponce" or expect food etc. for free

freeloader one who expects to gain for free

freeway, multi-lane highway, expressway motorway

freight train goods train

freight truck goods truck

French fries/fries chips

French toast eggy bread

frisky lively, mischievous

front desk (hotel) reception

front desk clerk receptionist

frosting (food) icing

furnace boiler

G

galoshes, rubber boots, gumboots wellington boots

gangway aisle

garage sale sometimes, "yard sale" – where people sell their junk! See UK "car boot sale"

garbage rubbish

garbage bag bin liner

garbage collector dustman

garbage/trash can dustbin/bin

garbage truck dust cart

garden (v.) to tend a garden

garter belt suspender belt

garburator (Canada), **garbage disposal unit** waste disposal unit

gas pedal accelerator

gas station filling station/petrol station (filling station works everywhere)

gasoline/gas petrol

gator southern US states, alligator

gear shift gear lever

general manager managing director/MD (varies according to nature of company)

German Shepherd dog, often known in UK as Alsation

gimp (sad) slang for someone who limps

girl, chick bird, lass (Scottish)

give me a break "do me a favour" ... don't bother me with that rubbish

given name Christian name, first name

giving the bird showing the middle finger, like UK flicking a "V" sign

glove compartment glove box (car)

go figure work it out for yourself

gofer factotum – someone who "goes for this, goes for that."

golf (v.) **/ golfing** to play golf / playing golf

golf cart golf buggy

golf shirt polo shirt

good driver discount no claims bonus

goofy a bit silly, off the wall

goose bumps goose pimples

gopher rodent common almost everywhere in North America, about the size of a rabbit

gotten got

grade (school)
class/form/year

grade school primary
and secondary school

grade crossing
(railroad) level crossing

Graham crackers
biscuits a little like the
UK's digestive biscuits

granola breakfast cereal
similar to muesli, except
ingredients are toasted

**green
onion/scallion/salad
onion** spring onion

green thumb green
fingers (means someone
is good at growing
plants!)

grits breakfast dish,
common in southern
states, made from ground
corn/maize

**grocery shopping,
groceries** food shopping

gross disgusting

gross out to disgust

ground (n. and v.)
(electricity) earth

ground (n.) (real
estate/property) land

ground (adj.)
**beef/pork/etc /
hamburger** (beef, pork
or other meat) mince

Groundhog Day
February 2nd ... when the
groundhog or
woodchuck, a large
rodent, decides if spring
is on its way or not

guy, man bloke

gyp (v.) to cheat

H

hair spray hair lacquer

hamburger, hamburger meat minced meat (nearly always beef) to be made into hamburgers

hamper basket, e.g. laundry basket

hang up (phone) ring off

hardware, hardware store ironmongery, ironmonger

harp (v.) to nag, bang on (slang)

haul tow

heavy cream double cream

hiccup hiccough

hick yokel, pleb

hickey love bite

highball long drink, usually of spirits and mixer

hillbilly, hoodlum yob, chav

hired hand worker

hobo tramp, homeless person

hockey ice hockey

hoedown party with dancing, especially with square dancing

Hogtown Toronto, Canada

hogwash nonsense

hokey cheesy, cheap

homemaker housewife

homogenized milk whole milk

honk (v.) hoot horn

hood bonnet (car)

hood smalltime criminal

hoodlum badly behaved person, usually young, vandal

hooky, hookey, to play to truant from school or other activity

hope chest (bride to be) bottom drawer

horny randy

horse puckey horse manure, stupid person

horse potooties horse manure, stupid person or situation (Canada)

hot stolen

hot dog frankfurter, usually served in appropriately shaped "bun" with relish and/or sauces

house phone landline

housebreak (pets) house train

housing project similar to council estate

huffy offended

Humidex (Canada) meteorological scale combining effects of heat and humidity

hunker down get on with it, keep a low profile

hunting (birds, deer, etc.) shooting

husky (adj.) chunky, stocky (person)

hydro (Canada except Alberta, Saskatchewan, and the Maritimes) electricity supply

I

IRS (Internal Revenue Service) UK equivalent is HMRC (Her Majesty's Revenue and Customs)

idiot, dumb-ass pillock, pratt

idle (car motor) tick over

impaired driver drunk driver

impatiens (plant) impatiens, Busy Lizzie

in back of behind

in heat on heat

in the hospital in hospital

income statement profit and loss account

incorporated company limited (company)

Indian burn Chinese burn

Indians/First Nation (people) American Indians

indict charge with crime, officially

"information" (phone) directory enquiries

insane, crazy mad

inside lane (highway) outside lane

installment plan hire purchase

insurance insurance, insurance cover

intermission (theater) interval

intersection crossroads
interstate main road, highway, serving two or more US states

inventory (business, retail) stock

investment bank merchant bank

Ivy League describes so called "top" US universities

J

jackhammer pneumatic drill

jail gaol (prison)

jalopy old car, old banger

jambalaya Louisiana dish of rice, vegetables and meat or fish, similar to Spanish paella

janitor caretaker/porter

jello (brand name – Jell-O) jelly (sweet)

jelly roll Swiss roll

jerk (n.) idiot

jetski sea-doo (Canada)

jock expert at sports or other activities

joint bar, café etc.

john (slang) toilet, also (slang) prostitute's client

"John Doe" "Joe Bloggs" – female equivalent "Jane Doe"

K

kabob kebab

keister bottom, backside

kerosene paraffin
(liquid)

kick-ass (adj.) strong,
forceful, important

kidding joking

klutz clumsy person

knock on wood
(expression re: "for luck")
touch wood

knock up render
pregnant

L

labor union trade union

ladybug (insect) ladybird

laid off (employment) redundant, made redundant

larceny theft

last name surname

latex paint emulsion paint

launder wash and iron

laundromat launderette

laundry washing (n.)

lawyer/attorney solicitor/barrister

lazy boy (from brand name) recliner chair

lazy Susan round, rotating food serving tray on one or more levels

leash (dog) lead (n.)

lemonade usually means home-made lemonade

levee bank to stop river flooding, dyke

license plate (car) number/registration plate, in most cases combines function of UK tax disc i.e. showing annual duty has been paid

lightning rod lightning conductor

lima bean broad bean

line/line up (n.) queue (n.)

line up/stand in line queue (v.)

links sausages, string of sausages

liquor/hard liquor spirits (drink)

liquor store off licence/wine merchant

listed company quoted company

liverwort liver sausage

living room sitting room / living room / lounge / drawing room / front room

lobby foyer

locomotive railway engine

long distance (phonecall) trunk call

longe (horses) lunge

loonie (Canadian) one Canadian dollar coin

lost and found lost property

lot (real estate) plot

lox smoked salmon

luggage baggage

luggage rack (car) roof rack

lumber (wood) timber

lunch pail lunch box

M

mad angry

mail (n. & v.) post
(n. & v.)

mail box pillar box/letter
box/post box

mailman postman

maître d (maître d'hotel)
head waiter

major in (main university
subject) study, read

make a right/left turn
turn right/left

make out get into
heaving petting, have sex

make reservation book
(v.)

math maths

max (v.) to push to
extreme limit, e.g. credit
card)

mean unkind

median (highway)
central reservation

melt sandwich, usually
open, topped with melted
cheese

menstrual period
period

merchandise trade
visible trade

mezzanine dress circle
in theatre, also
intermediate section

between two main floors of building

Midwest actually north central states, roughly (and arguably) from Ohio in the east to the Dakotas in the west, the Great Lakes to the north and Kansas and Missouri in the south

MILITARY : US AIR FORCE RANKS

Airman Basic
Airman
Airman First Class
Senior Airman
Staff Sergeant
Technical Sergeant
Master Sergeant
Master Sergeant (Note Diamond)
Senior Master Sergeant
Senior Master
Sergeant (Note Diamond)
Chief Master Sergeant
Chief Master
Sergeant (Note Diamond)
Command Chief Master

Sergeant
Chief Master Sergeant of the Air Force
Second Lieutenant
First Lieutenant
Captain
Major
Lieutenant Colonel
Colonel
Brigadier General
Major General
Lieutenant General
General Air Force Chief of Staff
General of the Air Force (wartime)

MILITARY: US ARMY RANKS

Private
Private 2
Private First Class
Specialist
Corporal
Sergeant
Staff Sergeant
Sergeant First Class
Master Sergeant
First Sergeant
Sergeant Major

Command Sergeant Major

Sergeant Major of the Army

Warrant Officer

Chief Warrant Officer 2

Chief Warrant Officer 3

Chief Warrant Officer 4

Chief Warrant Officer 5

Second Lieutenant

First Lieutenant

Captain

Major

Lieutenant Colonel

Colonel

Brigadier General

Major General

Lieutenant General

General

General of the Army (wartime)

MILITARY: US NAVY RANKS

Seaman Recruit

Seaman Apprentice

Seaman

Petty Officer 3rd Class

Petty Officer 2nd Class

Petty Officer 1st Class

Chief Petty Officer

Senior Chief Petty Officer

Master Chief Petty Officer

Fleet / Command Master Chief Petty Officer

Master Chief Petty Officer of the Navy

Chief Warrant Officer 2

Chief Warrant Officer 3

Chief Warrant Officer 4

Chief Warrant Officer 5

Ensign

Lieutenant Junior Grade

Lieutenant

Lieutenant Commander

Commander

Captain

Rear Admiral (lower half)

Rear Admiral (upper half)

Vice Admiral

Admiral Chief of Naval Operations /Commandant of the CG

Fleet Admiral

mimosa (drink) bucks fizz

molasses black treacle

mom mum (short form for "mother")

mom and pop family-run, e.g. business

momentarily soon

monitor (school) prefect

monkey wrench spanner (adjustable)

moonshine illegally made alcoholic drink

mortician undertaker, funeral director

motor (vehicle) engine

Mountain States states located (roughly) either side of the Rocky Mountain range

movie, motion picture film (n.)

movie theater, movie house cinema, "the pictures"

moving removals, moving house

muffler silencer (car)

MPV (multi-purpose vehicle) / van people carrier

mums (flowers) chrysanthemums

municipal government council/local authority

municipal judge magistrate

muscle car high-performance road car

music notes:
double whole note breve
whole note semibreve
half note minim
quarter note crotchet

eighth note quaver
sixteenth note
semiquaver
thirty-second note
demisemiquaver

muss (v.) mess up

mutual fund unit trust

muumuu flowing
Hawaiian dress

N

nail polish nail varnish, nail lacquer

Nanaimo bar (Canada) sweet treat of custard, chocolate, etc

national/public holiday bank holiday

nauseous nauseated

neck (v.), **play tonsil hockey** snog (v.), heavy kissing

nerd geek, social misfit

New England states in far north-east – Vermont, New Hampshire, Maine, Massachusetts, Rhode Island, Connecticut

Newfie (Canada, slang) person from Newfoundland and Labrador

newsstand bookstall

nickel 5 cent coin

nightstand bedroom table

nightstick (police) truncheon

nipple (on baby's bottle) teat

normalcy normality

notary public commissioner for oaths

nuke slang for heating something in a microwave oven, also general term for "destroy"

number key hash key

ocean sea, seaside

odometer mileometer (both terms widely used)

on the fritz broken

on the weekend at the weekend

one-on-one one-to-one

one-way ticket single ticket

operating room (medical, OR) theatre (medical, operating)

optician optician (dispensing)

optometrist optician (ophthalmic)

orchestra seats (theatre) stalls

organ meat offal

orient (v.) orientate

ornery difficult, uncooperative

out west (USA) west of the Rockies – (Canada) Manitoba, Saskatchewan, Alberta & British Columbia

outlet/socket point/power point/socket

oven mitt, pot holder oven cloth/gloves

over easy eggs fried lightly on both sides

overalls dungarees (both terms can be used everywhere)

overpass fly-over

overseas abroad

overhead overheads

P

Pacific North West
Oregon and Washington
state

pacifier (baby) dummy

pack (e.g. candy, potato
chips, etc**)** packet

package parcel

paddle (table tennis) bat

paid-in surplus share
premium

pail bucket

paint (horses) coloured
(i.e. horses coloured
white plus one or two
other colours)

pan handle long, narrow
part of state e.g. north-
west Florida, also to beg
for money (using pan to
collect!)

panties (girls') knickers

pantry larder

pants trousers

pantyhose tights

paper towels kitchen
paper

parade carnival

paraffin paraffin wax

parentheses (writing)
brackets

parking brake
handbrake

parking garage multi-storey car park

parking lights sidelights

parking lot car park

parkway pleasantly landscaped road or highway

party (v.) celebrate

pass (v.)(highway) overtake

patsy scapegoat

pavement road surface

peekaboo (child's game) peebo

penitentiary prison

pepper/coffee grinder pepper/coffee mill

period (punctuation) full stop

person-to-person call personal call

pesky irritating, annoying

Philly Philadelphia

physical therapy physiotherapy

physical therapist physiotherapist

phone booth telephone kiosk/callbox

pick pickaxe

pig pen pigsty

pinkie little finger

pissed angry, pissed off

pit stone (fruit)

pitcher jug

plaid tartan

plastic wrap/Saran wrap (brand name) clingfilm

Plexiglass Perspex

poison ivy also poison oak, poison sumac – wild plants containing serious skin irritants

pollywog/tadpole tadpole

pop (v.) to open

pop (Canada) non-alcoholic fizzy drink

popsicle iced lolly

pork rinds (food) pork scratchings

porterhouse steak sirloin steak

pot holder oven glove

poutine (Canada) Originally French Canadian – chips (French fries), cheese curds and gravy

powder room ladies' toilet

powdered/ confectioner's sugar icing sugar

power outage power cut

prairie dog squirrel-like large rodent found mainly in western states and Canadian provinces

prenatal antenatal

precinct district (district can be used everywhere)

preppie (from US private high school) upper class person

presently now, at present

president (of business) chairman

prime rate (finance) base rate

principal (school) headmaster/headmistress /headteacher

private school (high school level) public school

prize drawing prize draw (competition, contest etc)

pruning shears secateurs

public/high school state primary school/state secondary school

pull-off, turn-out lay-by

pump (shoe) court shoe

purse handbag

putter (v.) to potter, e.g. around garden

quarter quarter of a dollar, i.e. 25 cent coin

quarter of quarter to (time, 15 minutes before hour)

quarterback (v.) and (n.) to lead, leader

quit stop (e.g. quit/stop smoking)

quotation marks (punctuation) inverted commas

R

RV (recreational vehicle), motorhome camper van/motor caravanette

raccoon lovable but destructive mammal, about the size of a small spaniel dog, common throughout most of North America

rag cloth, duster

railroad railway

raincheck postponement

raincoat mackintosh/mac

raise (in pay) rise

rambunctious wild, boisterous

rappel abseil

real estate property

realtor, real estate broker estate agent

ream out tell off, admonish

recess (school) break

red hair ginger hair

redneck derogatory term for working class man, usually rural

reform school Borstal

relevancy relevance

remodel renovate (e.g. house, kitchen)

rent (v.) let (v.) (as in homes/property)

rental car hire car

restroom public convenience/toilets

résumé CV (curriculum vitae)

ride (n.) lift given in car, etc

ride (v.) to travel in or on

ring up enter into cash register

rinky-dink cheap, poor quality

roast (n.) (meat) joint for roasting

rock garden rockery

rocks ice cubes

roller coaster big dipper (both terms used everywhere)

romaine lettuce cos lettuce

room mate flat mate

roomer lodger

rooster cockerel

root beer fizzy drink flavoured with sassafras etc., usually non-alcoholic but alcoholic versions exist

round trip ticket return ticket

rubber contraceptive/condom (may be confused with UK "eraser")

rubber band elastic band

rubbing alcohol surgical spirit

rug toupée, wig

rummage sale jumble sale

run (n.) (pantyhose, nylons) ladder (tights, stockings)

run (v.) (e.g. for public office) stand (v.)

runaway ramp (highway) escape road

running shoes/sneakers gym shoes/plimsolls/tennis shoes/trainers

rutabaga/Swedish turnip swede

S

S&H (shipping & handling) P&P (postage & packaging)

SMS text (as in smartphone)

SUV (sports utility vehicle) 4WD/off-roader (vehicle)

sack, hit the go to bed

sales clerk, counter clerk shop assistant

saltine salted biscuit or cracker

sand box sand pit

sasquatch Big Foot, Yeti, mythical creature in far north-west of US and far west of Canada

savings & loan association building society

scab blackleg/scab (person who won't conform to union)

scarf (v.) to eat quickly

scavenger hunt (children's game) treasure hunt

schedule time-table

schmuck idiot

school also used to describe university and other tertiary education

Scotch Scotch whisky

Scotch tape Sellotape (both brand names)

scratch pad scribbling pad/block

screw anchor Rawlplug

screw over swindle

second floor first floor

sedan saloon car

seeing eye dog guide dog

semester term (academic)

senior citizen, senior pensioner

server (restaurant) waiter/waitress

service station services, motorway services

set the table lay the table

sewer pipe drain

sexually aroused, horny randy

shade (window) blind (both terms widely used)

shaved (horse, dog, etc.) clipped

sheers net curtains

sherbet ice/sorbet

shill (n. and v.) (n.) fake customer who tries to upsell real ones (v.) the act of doing this

shingles (building) roof tiles

ship (v.) to send, transport (v.)

shoot the breeze to chat, gossip

shopping cart shopping trolley

shopping mall shopping centre

shorts, jockey shorts briefs/underpants

shot (injection) jab

shoulder (road) hard shoulder

shredded (coconut) desiccated

shrimps prawns

shuck (v.) to remove outer leaves etc. e.g. from corn on the cob

shyster a tricky or criminal practitioner, usually a lawyer or accountant

sick, to be (unwell) to be ill, poorly

sideburns sideboards (hair)

sidewalk pavement/footpath

silver, sterling (esp. Canada) silver, solid

silverware/flatware cutlery

sink (small) basin, washbasin, handbasin

sirloin steak rump steak

skillet frying pan

skim milk skimmed milk

skip (v.) leave out, avoid, e.g. "I skipped lunch today"

slate (v.) insult, criticize

slaughterhouse abattoir

sled sleigh

sleep in (sleep late) lie in

slice rasher (bacon)

sling shot catapult

slot machine fruit machine

smart alec cheeky person

smartass know-it-all

smoked herring (food) kipper

snit (n.), **snitty** (adj.) sulk, sulky

snow birds people from south-east Canada and north-east USA who migrate to Florida for the winter season – also western Canadians and (north)west Americans spending winter in Arizona, California, Mexico, etc.

snowmobile ski-doo (Canada)

so long goodbye, cheerio

soccer football/soccer

social security number national insurance number

soda (USA) sweet fizzy drink

soda cracker cream cracker

sooner, (e.g.) I would rather, (e.g.) I would

sorrel (horses, colour) chestnut

southpaw left handed person, especially in boxing

space heater gas or electric fire

specialist (medical) consultant (medical)

spool of thread cotton reel

sprouts usually means alfalfa or bean sprouts

spunk bravery

squash (vegetable) marrow

standard/stick shift (car gears) manual

station wagon estate car

steal pinch, nick

stoplights traffic lights

storm windows secondary glazing

stingy/tightwad mean

stock share

stock dividend / stock split bonus / capitalisation issue

stockholder shareholder

stockholders' equity shareholders' equity

stoop small porch

stove/range cooker / range cooker

straight (undiluted alcoholic drink) neat

street car tram

strep throat throat infection due to

streptococcus, "tonsillitis"

string beans runner beans

strip mall parade of shops

stroller pushchair

studio apartment bedsit

study (for examinations) revise

sub-division housing estate

substitute teacher supply teacher

subway tube/underground/metro

sunny side up eggs fried on one side only

super fine sugar castor sugar

sure (can mean) yes

suspenders (to hold up pants) braces

sweater (clothing) jersey/jumper/sweater/pullover

swiffer (to clean) use of brand name wipes to clean

switchback hairpin bend

T

table (v.) to assign a motion to a later date

tacky seedy, cheap and nasty

taffy (candy) toffee

tailor made bespoke

take a raincheck postpone

take the fifth means right to remain silent in order to avoid – potentially – incriminating yourself

tea cart tea trolley

tear down (construction) demolish

teetor-totter see-saw

teleprompter Autocue (brand name)

teller cashier (bank)

Texas gate, cattle guard cattle grid

Thanksgiving public holiday the 2nd Monday of October (Canada) and the 4th Thursday of November (USA)

Thermos (brand name) vacuum flask / flask

thread (sewing) cotton

threads clothes

throw up (vomit) be sick

through (I'm through doing this) (I have) finished

thruway motorway bypassing congested area

thumb tack drawing pin

tic-tac-toe (game) naughts/noughts and crosses

Timmie (Canada) Tim Horton's coffee house, place or product. Similar to Starbucks.

to go, take out (food) takeaway (also "carryout," Scotland)

toboggan/sled sledge

toilet/washroom/bathroom loo / toilet

toll free (phone) freephone

tool (v.) to drive car, usually fast

toonie (Canadian) Canadian two dollar coin

toothpick cocktail stick, toothpick

top (car) roof/hood

top round (beef) silverside

total (v.)(car wreck, from "total loss") write off (from "insurance write-off")

townhouse terraced house

track and field (sport) athletics

tractor trailer articulated lorry

traffic circle, rotary (road) roundabout

traffic/stop lights/signals traffic lights

trail footpath, bridleway (horses)

trailer hitch/tow hitch towbar

trailer, mobile home caravan

trailer park caravan site

trailer truck, transport articulated lorry/artic

training wheels (for child's bicycle) stabilizers

tramp woman of loose morals

transmission gearbox

transportation, transit transport (n.)

trash rubbish, garbage

trash can rubbish bin

Treasury bonds gilt-edged stock (gilts)

trial lawyer barrister

truck lorry

truck stop lorry park

trunk (car) boot

turkey failed product, business or activity, idiot

turn lights (car) indicators

turnpike tool road

turtle neck (sweater) polo neck

tush bottom, backside

tuxedo dinner jacket

Twin Cities Minneapolis and St Paul, Minnesota

two weeks fortnight

U

undergraduates:
freshman 1st year
sophomore 2nd year
junior 3rd year
senior 4th year

underpass subway

undershirt vest

underwear smalls

unlisted (phone number) ex-directory

upscale upmarket

V

vacation, holidays
holiday

vacationer holiday
maker

vacuum / vacuum clean
(v.) Hoover (v., brand
name for appliance)

vacuum cleaner Hoover
(n., brand name)

vaudeville
(entertainment) music
hall

vest waistcoat

vet/veteran veteran

vet/veterinarian
vet/veterinary surgeon

vice president
(company) director

visit, visit with (n. and
v.) social time / spend
social time with one or
more others, e.g. "visit
with my mother"

wakeup call alarm call

wakeup call (to give) knock up (NB: "Knock up" also can mean to get a woman pregnant)

walk-up used to describe a 2 or more storey building that doesn't have a lift (elevator)

walker Zimmer frame

wall-to-wall carpet fitted carpet

warm up (tennis) knock up

wasp/yellow jacket (insect) wasp

waste (v.) to kill

water heater (electric) immersion heater

wax paper grease-proof paper

weed whacker (gardening) strimmer

welfare (Govt. help for low income families) benefits / on benefits

wetback derogatory term for illegal immigrant inbound from Mexico

whiskey usually means bourbon

wiener (food) frankfurter

wifebeater men's vest or sleeveless T-shirt

windshield (car) windscreen

Windy City, The Chicago

wire telegram (not used much these days!)

wiseguy know-it-all

with cream/milk or without? (coffee/tea) black or white?

wintergreen popular flavouring for chewing gum, mouthwash etc., derived mostly from *Gaultheria* plants

woodchuck another name for groundhog, a large rodent

workshop/shop (car maintenance etc.) garage

wrench spanner

write write to

XYZ

Xerox (brand name) photocopier (machine)

yam sweet potato

yard, back yard garden (n.)

yellow jacket another name for wasp

yellow light (traffic lights) amber light

yield (on roads/highways) give way

zee (letter Z) zed

zero naught/nought

zap slang for heating something in a microwave oven, also general term for "destroy"

zip nothing

zipper zip

zip code (USA) post code (UK) / postal code (Canada)

zucchini (vegetable) courgette / baby marrow

ABOUT SUZE

Canadian born Suzan St Maur (a.k.a. "Suze") was transported to the UK when a child and despite resultant cultural challenges managed to leave British secondary school with a couple of "A" levels and no talent for anything other than writing, so her career options were fairly clear cut.

She attended and graduated from the then-famous Watford Art School advertising writing course and worked in London ad agencies as a copywriter for a few years, before deciding she was far too bolshie to be an employee and so became a freelancer.

While comfortably paying her mortgage and bills her work took off into the areas of business theatre and corporate video, in which disciplines she became the Grandma Moses of corporate script and speechwriting for many years.

Suze also developed useful skills as a conference and video producer, largely in emergencies caused by the actual practitioners' bunking off through illness, drunkenness, excessive use of recreational substances, etc. It's amazing how fast you can learn to do a job if the person who should be doing it is in la-la-land and the client expects top performance, right now...

These days Suze concentrates on printed/electronic words. She enjoys consulting, writing, editing for and coaching clients in addition to running her other business interests, writing her own books, blogs and articles, plus giving workshops, radio interviews, etc., on how to make your writing more successful.

It was this work which inspired her to create HowToWriteBetter.net so she could share her experience and skills with an even wider audience.

SUZE'S PUBLISHED/ CONTRACTED BOOKS INCLUDE:

- **The Jewellery Book** (with Norbert Streep) (Magnum)
- **The Home Safety Book** (Jill Norman Books)
- **The A to Z of Video and AV Jargon** (Routledge)
- **Writing Words That Sell** (with John Butman) (Management Books 2000)
- **Writing Your Own Scripts and Speeches** (McGraw Hill)
- **The Horse Lover's Joke Book** (Kenilworth Press)
- **Powerwriting**: the hidden skills you need to transform your business writing (Prentice Hall Business)
- **Canine Capers: over 350 jokes to make your tail wag** (Kenilworth Press)
- **The Food Lover's Joke Book** (ItsCooking.com)
- **Get Yourself Published** (LeanMarketing Press)
- **The MAMBA Way To Make Your Words Sell** (LeanMarketing Press)
- **The Easy Way To Be Brilliant At Business Writing** (LeanMarketing Press)
- **Wedding Speeches For Women** (How To Books)
- **The Country Lover's Joke Book** (Merlin Unwin)
- **The A to Z of Wedding Worries** (How To Books)

- **How To Get Married In Green** (How To Books)
- **Planning A Winter Wedding** (How To Books)
- **How To Write Winning Nonfiction** (Bookshaker)
- **The A to Z Of Wedding Wisdom** (How To Books)
- **The Pony Lover's Joke Book** (Kenilworth Press)
- **Banana Skin Words and how not to slip on them**
- **The English Language Joke Book** (HTWB)
- **Business Writing Made Easy** (Bookshaker)
- **English To English: The A to Z of British-American**
- **Translations** (Bookshaker)
- **Super Speeches** (HTWB, due 2012)
- **How To Sell Yourself In Writing** (HTWB, due 2012)
- **How To Smile Through Cancer** (HTWB, due 2012)
- **Out By The Roots** (Discovered Authors, due 2013)

PERSONAL STUFF

Suze has lived in the UK since she was a child. Her parents settled near Milton Keynes, Bucks and although Suze lived and worked in London for many years she returned to the Milton Keynes area in the later 1980s. Her dad ran a local newspaper in Milton Keynes and that probably set the wheels turning where her writing is concerned. Her first published effort (in dad's paper of course!) when she was 15, was the children's saga of "Whipley and Booley" the hooligan bears.

Suze's London days were "work hard, play hard" and Fulham, where she lived, will never be quite the same again. While there, for two years she had her own chat and music show on Charing Cross Hospital Radio and enjoyed that thoroughly. She also got involved in politics and helped with communications for one of the major parties at Westminster, as well as standing as a candidate in a London borough council election.

Her son Tom was born in 1992 and after a "gap year" working for a major bank, as of September 2011 attends The Leicester Business School/De Montfort University (UK) reading business management, economics and econometrics. Until recently he was a drummer in various heavy metal rock bands, most of

which would rehearse at the family home ... noisy but good fun.

Apart from work, Suze is a keen horsewoman and helps at horse shows – specifically, dressage competitions - on weekends. Unable to ride for some years due to health problems (see below) she is now planning a horsey comeback – it's just a matter of finding a horse that's quiet enough, strong enough (and possibly foolish enough) to carry her.

In 2003 Suze developed cancer of the bladder which was treated "conservatively" (i.e. with chemotherapy and immunotherapy and only minor surgery) until 2010 when her bladder, along with various other bits and pieces, was removed. She now takes great pride in being able to void her urostomy bag in places far less inconvenient than ladies' toilets – especially out in the wilds when helping at a horse show...

Not long after nursing her mother, who had terminal cancer, at home for 7 months while still running the business and parenting son Tom on her own, Suze developed a cancer of the breast – unrelated to the bladder cancer. She had a mastectomy in 2005 and underwent chemotherapy which resulted in a number of funny stories about wigs, prostheses and much more which Suze still writes about on her other blog, CancerComic-Strip. Currently she is developing a book based on the blog which she hopes to sell and donate some of the proceeds to Macmillan, her favourite UK cancer charity.

These days Suze is Vice Chair of the Milton Keynes Cancer Patient Partnership which consists of volunteers like her, as users of cancer services, working with the healthcare professionals to improve the services delivered locally, regionally and nationally. Suze works on communications as well as peer review, environmental audits, training, and other projects.

Apart from her son and her family in Canada and Belgium (her mother was Belgian, hence Suze speaks French fluently) Suze's great love is animals – particularly horses (see above), dogs and cats. She has had various rescued dogs and cats over the years and as many of her friends know, she's a soft touch for a "hard luck" story! However she did turn down one recent rehoming request – for a rabbit. With two dogs and three hard-hunting cats, its life expectancy would have been less than 10 minutes...

Suze with LaWoof the Gordon Setter and Ozzie the "Mexican Mouse Hound" a.k.a. mongrel

BIBLIOGRAPHY AND FURTHER READING

By Anthea Bickerton:
- ***American-English, English-American: A Two-way Glossary of Words in Daily Use on Both Sides of the Atlantic***

By Dileri Borunda Johnston:
- ***Speak American: A Survival Guide to the Language and Culture of the U.S.A***

By Jane Walmsley:
- ***Brit-think, Ameri-think: A Transatlantic Survival Guide***

By Jeremy Smith:
- ***Bum Bags and Fanny Packs***

By Jonathon Green:
- ***Green's Dictionary of Slang [3 Vol Set]***
- ***Crooked Talk: Five Hundred Years of the Language of Crime***
- ***Chambers' Slang Dictionary***

- ***The Slang Thesaurus***
- ***The Dictionary of Contemporary Slang***
- ***The Dictionary of New Words***
- ***The Cassell Dictionary of Slang***
- ***Newspeak: a Dictionary of Jargon***
- **(plus numerous others!)**

ONLINE RESOURCES

- www.forces.gc.ca
- www.airforce.gov.au
- www.airforce.mil.nz
- www.MilitaryFactory.com
- www.Army.mod.uk
- www.EnglishClub.com
- www.wikipedia.org

Made in the USA
Lexington, KY
03 September 2014